Table of Contents

Introduction

Growing psilocybin mushrooms has been getting popular in recent years. More and more studies are being conducted regarding the therapeutic value of psilocybin and its effectiveness in treating depression or other psychological disorders. Some states such as California or Colorado had initiatives that aimed to legalize psilocybin mushrooms and, while the mushrooms are illegal, the spores or grow kits needed to grow magic mushrooms are legal in most parts of the world.

People who want to know how to grow magic mushrooms (for research purposes, of course) might find the task daunting. It's actually quite easy, especially if you're growing shrooms from grow kits. If you want to do it yourself with your own psilocybin spores, you can also grow mushrooms with the PF Tek method. This guide will show you how to grow magic mushrooms through both methods.

Magic Mushrooms

Magic mushrooms are a variety of mushroom known for producing strong psychedelic effects when ingested. Mushrooms are a fungus, meaning they grow from spores that establish mycelium networks in the ground or decaying plant material, such as old logs. When the conditions are just right, a fungus will bloom similar to a flower. These blooms are the mushrooms that we harvest.

The most common varieties of psychoactive mushrooms fall under the Psilocybin genus.This genus encompasses over 200 varieties of mushrooms, all of which contain psilocybin, the main active compound responsible for producing psychoactive effects. There are other varieties of mushrooms which also produce psychedelic effects, such as the fly amanita.

Origin

The exact origins of magic mushrooms is highly debated. However, one thing is for sure; the exact origin of psychoactive mushrooms dates back a lot further than we once thought. Many people believe the use of hallucinogenic substances took off in the 1960s. However, archaeological evidence shows that some of these substances have been used by human civilizations for thousands of years.

In 1992, Italian ethnobotanist Giorgio Samorini found a painted rock mural depicting mushrooms in Tassili n'Ajjer, a mountain range in the Algerian section of the Sahara Desert. The mural dates back to between 7000 to 9000 BCE. The mushrooms depicted in the mural are speculated to be psilocybe mairei, a psychoactive mushroom species native to Algeria and Morocco.

There is also a large body of evidence suggesting the use of entheogens by ancient cultures in mesoamerica, especially among the Aztecs. Some of the most detailed references to the use of psychoactive plants by the Aztecs come from The Florentine Codex, a comprehensive ethnographic study in Mesoamerica from the 16th century by Spanish Franciscan friar Bernardino de Sahagún.

De Sahagún was a missionary and was set on evangelizing the indigenous people of Mesoamerica. Sahagún is quoted as describing The Florentine Codex as an explanation of the "divine, or rather idolatrous, human, and natural things of New Spain".

Sahagún's work comprises of 2,400 pages organized into twelve books and provides detailed insight into how the Aztecs used psychoactive plants as part of their spiritual rituals. Some of the plants they used include ololiuqui (a species of morning glory), peyote, and a species of psilocybin mushroom.

The Aztecs referred to mushrooms as teonanácatl, which literally translates to "god mushroom." The act of taking mushrooms was known as monanacahuia, meaning to "mushroom oneself". Sahagún, as well as other prominent missionaries of the time (such as Toribio de Benavente Motolinia, one of the famous Twelve Apostles of Mexico) described how the Aztecs would drink chocolate and eat the mushrooms with honey.

In the Florentine Codex, Sahagún writes: "At the very first, mushrooms had been served...They ate no more food; they only drank chocolate during the night. And they ate the mushrooms with honey. When the mushrooms took effect on them, then they danced, then they wept. But some, while still in command of their senses, entered and sat there by the house on their seats; they did no more, but only sat there nodding."

It is also possible that the Maya, an indigenous people of Central America with civilisations dating back to 2000 BCE, used psychoactive substances such as mushrooms prior to the Aztecs (whose civilisations date back to the 14th century). However, there is significantly less evidence to support this hypothesis. The Maya were an indigenous people of Central America who inhabited modern-day Yucatan, Quintana Roo, Campeche,

Tabasco, and Chiapas in Mexico, as well as areas through Guatemala, Belize, El Salvador and Honduras.

Maya Magic Mushroom

The first settled villages and earliest developments in agriculture in these areas took place between 8000 and 2000 BCE. The first Mayan civilisations were built between 2000 BCE and 250 AD. Most of the evidence suggesting that the Maya used psychoactive substances come from rock art and rare examples of residues of substances recovered from ceramic containers. Some of the substances traced back to the Mayas include tobacco, water lily, morning glory, and Psilocybe mexicana.

The most cited archaeological evidence used to support the argument that Mayas used psychoactive mushrooms is a collection of carved "mushroom stones." These stone sculptures, interpretations of mushrooms, have been found at many archeological sites and traced back to the Maya culture. However, there is a lack of consensus on whether these interpretations are accurate and, if so, whether they prove as evidence that the Mayans did, in fact, use psychoactive mushrooms.

The use of psychoactive mushrooms isn't unique to Africa and the Americas; it has also been linked back to Europe. In 2011, scientists discovered the Selva Pascuala cave mural near the town of Villar del Humo in Spain. The mural, dated back to roughly 6000 BCE, depicts a large bull as well as 13 small mushroom-like objects. Scientists took great interest in these mushrooms, claiming they could be depictions of Psilocybe hispanica, a local species of psychoactive mushroom.

Psilocybe hispanica has a bell-shaped cap topped with a dome and lacks a annulus (a ring around the stalk). The objects in the Selva Pascuala mural are very similar to these mushrooms and even feature a combination of both straight and curved stems, as is common in this species of mushroom.

As we mentioned earlier, there is no exact answer as to where magic mushrooms originated from. However, there is significant historical and archaeological evidence proving that psychoactive mushrooms have long been used by humans for a variety of spiritual and religious purposes.

How do Mushrooms Grow

One of the most exciting things about growing your own mushrooms is intimately learning the mushroom lifecycle.

Mushrooms are really the fruiting bodies of the fungus, analogous to the fruits of a tree.

The fruiting bodies grow from mycelium, the vegetative part of the mushroom which can be thought of as the underground fruit-bearing tree. Mycelium is constituted of white, thread-like filaments called hyphae. They originate from fungal spores, the tiny "seeds" released by the fruiting bodies that are responsible for initiating the mushroom reproduction processes under suitable environmental conditions (more on these conditions later).

The mycelium grows on an inoculated (spore-infused) substrate until it fully colonizes the medium. The substrate is the organic matter environment that contains nutrients and water that the fungus uses to grow its mycelial networks in the colonization stage and, later, its fruiting bodies in the fruiting stage. Under the right growth conditions, fruiting bodies are produced in short bursts known as "flushes."

Where do Magic Mushrooms Grow Naturally

Psilocybin mushrooms (of which there are over 200 species) can be found on every major continent. In general, they flourish in the meadows, pastures, and woods of tropical and subtropical regions. Depending on the species in question, they can be found growing on dung or in damp, shady regions. Regions with wood chips, rotting logs, or soil rich in plant debris are particularly suitable for growth.

Once the mushroom spores land on the optimal medium, it takes four crucial factors to stimulate fruiting body growth:

- Humidity. Mushrooms are over 90% water, so high humidity environments (above 90%) are key for proper growth. High humidity allows the mycelium to retain adequate moisture levels and encourages healthy "pinning." Pinning refers to the first recognizable mass of hyphae that will become the fruiting body.

- Light. Since mushrooms don't produce their own nutrients from the sun as plants do, they don't require direct sunlight. Indirect sunlight, however, signals to the mycelium to stop colonizing and start fruiting.

- Temperature. Temperature needs vary depending on the mushroom variety, but in general, a temperature between 60-90F is necessary for fruiting body growth. Too high of a temperature desiccates the mycelium and fruiting bodies, while too low of a temperature will thwart mycelial growth.

- Fresh air exchange. Just like humans, mushrooms breathe oxygen. For this reason, they require constant fresh air exchange to grow properly. Low levels of carbon dioxide are a signal for the mycelium to start producing fruiting bodies. If the carbon dioxide levels are too high, this will skew fruiting body growth by producing long stems and small caps.

Indoor magic mushroom growing techniques seek to imitate the natural growing conditions that the mushrooms are subjected to in the wild. Armed with an understanding of the environmental conditions that mushrooms need to grow well, let's dive into indoor cultivation.

What You Need to Grow Magic Mushrooms at Home

This grow guide is based on a growing method called PF Tek. This method was originally developed in the early 1990s by Robert Mcpherson, also known as "Psylocybe Fanaticus." This method streamlined indoor cultivation, making it easy, inexpensive, and reliable for beginners.

Basic Materials You Will Need

One of the major advantages of the PF Tek method is that the materials needed are cheap and widely available online or in grocery and gardening stores. Here, we will outline the basic materials needed to get started.

- Substrate materials
- Spore syringe
- Organic brown rice flour (purchased or made at home by grinding brown rice in a coffee grinder)
- Vermiculite
- Water
- Gypsum (helps stabilize the pH, adds nutrients for the mycelium, and prevents the substrate from clumping)
- ½ pint wide-mouthed canning jars with lids (Ball or Kerr jars work well)
- Mixing bowl
- Measuring cup
- Spoon
- Heavy-duty aluminum foil
- Hammer
- 3 penny nail
- Small towel or extra jar lids
- Pressure cooker or large pot with a tight-fitting lid
- Fruiting chamber materials
- Clear, rectangular plastic tote (70 quart totes work well)

- Coarse Perlite

- Colander/strainer

- Electric drill with a ¼" drill bit

- Measuring tape

- Sharpie

- 6500K "daylight" fluorescent bulb

- Sterile working materials

- 70% Isopropyl Alcohol

- Lighter

- Surface disinfectant

- Latex gloves

- Dust/surgical mask

Magic Mushroom Spores

Magic mushroom spores, the most important piece of the grow, are needed to inoculate the substrate. Spore syringes can be purchased from reputable suppliers and are sold legally for "microscopy reasons." A syringe typically contains 20mL of spore solution, enough to inoculate twenty 1/2-pint jars of the substrate.

While a wide variety of species are available, Psilocybe cubenesis spores are generally regarded as the best species to work with as a beginner. Let's take a look at some of the most popular strains of P. cubensis.

B+ P. cubensis

Originating from Florida, B+ is by and large one of the most popular strains for beginners. It produces very large, good-quality yields and has a fast colonization rate. In addition, it tends to be less finicky with respect to environmental conditions like light, temperature, and substrate type.

Golden Teacher P. cubensis

Golden Teachers originated from a farm in Georgia, and are among the most cultivated strains today. They generally don't fruit as fast as some other strains, but they grow well in suboptimal conditions and produce a large amount of medium-sized fruiting bodies.

Penis Envy P. cubensis

A purported mutant of an Amazonian cubensis strain, Penis Envy is a renowned strain known for its high potency and unmistakably phallic appearance. It is known to be a steady, slow grower, but with the payoff of a powerful trip in the end.

Steps for Growing Magic Mushrooms from Spores

Taking a high-level overview, the PF Tek method involves preparing a substrate mixture of brown rice flour, water, and vermiculite. The vermiculite adds extra space to the grain mixture, allowing the mycelium to extend across the substrate and colonize effectively.

Once the substrate is prepared, it is loaded into jars and topped with a filter of dry vermiculite. The mushroom spores are then injected into each of the jars under sterile conditions. The inoculated substrate is then gradually colonized by the mycelium over a few weeks.

The colonized substrate is then relocated to a fruiting chamber that emulates natural growing conditions found in the wild. Here, the mushrooms will grow over the course of another week or two with consistent misting and fanning.

Step #1: Preparation

1. Preparing the jars:

Using a hammer and nail, create 4 evenly-spaced holes on the 5 jar lids. Make the hole near the rim, close to the edges. Disinfect the hammer and nail by wiping with 70% isopropyl alcohol prior to puncturing the lids.

2. Preparing the substrate:

The basic substrate recipe calls for 1 part brown rice flour-2 parts vermiculite-1 part water.

In the mixing bowl, combine 2 cups of vermiculite, 1 tablespoon of gypsum, and 1 cup of water. Mix well.

Add 1 cup of brown rice flour to the mixture. Mix everything well again.

3. Fill the jars:

Add the mixture into the 5 canning jars equally, filling to ½ inch below the rims. Be sure not to compress the mix into the jars. You want the substrate to be loose and airy.

Using a paper towel, wipe away any moisture or substrate mixture that may be present on the remaining ½ inch of jar space. Then, sterilize this space by wiping with 70% iso alcohol.

Top off the jars with dry vermiculite. This vermiculite layer acts as an extra barrier against opportunistic mold and germs.

4. Sterilize the substrate:

Note: At this stage, the substrate mixture is contaminated with mold spores and bacteria, which would outcompete the mycelium if left inside. We must, therefore, sterilize the substrate before inoculating the substrate with the mushroom spores.

Screw on the lids and cover the top with heavy-duty aluminum foil. The foil prevents any moisture from entering the jars during the sterilization process.

Before placing the jars in the pressure cooker or pot, you want to make sure the bottom of the jars do not make direct contact with the base of the pressure cooker or pot. To elevate the jars, place a small, thin towel on the base, and arrange the jars on top of that. Alternatively, add jar lid rings to the base of the pan to elevate the jars from the base.

Add cold water to the pot. The water level should be almost halfway up the side of the jars, a few inches from the base.

Bring the pot to a slow boil. Place the tight-fitting lid on and let steam for 90 minutes. Be sure the jars are upright throughout the process.

For the pressure cooker: Once the jars are arranged inside, set it to 15 PSI. Heat it on high until pressure is reached, then reduce heat and keep it in pressure for 1 hour.

Once the 60 or 90 minutes is up (for the pressure cooker or pot, respectively), turn off the heat and let them cool for 8-10 hours. Don't open up the pressure cooker or pot until this is done.

Step #2: Inoculation

1. Preparatory sanitary measures:

When the jars have cooled (8-10 hours later), open up the pot or pressure cooker and move the sterilized jars to a room with minimal airflow, such as a bathroom.

Thoroughly wash your hands and arms with soap and water, then put on the gloves and mask.

Now, flame-sterilize the syringe's needle with the lighter. Be sure to cover the length of the needle by moving the flame back and forth. Sterilize until it glows red hot, but be sure to avoid the part of the needle nearest to the plastic base of the syringe.

2. Inject the spores:

Remove the aluminum foil lid from the first jar. Rub your gloved hands down with 70% isopropyl alcohol and wait for it to evaporate.

Shake the syringe well, then insert the needle all the way into one of the holes. Tilt the syringe so the needle tip touches the side of the jar.

Inject approximately ¼ cc (¼ mL) of spore solution.

Repeat for the other three holes, totaling about 1cc of spore solution per jar. Be sure to sterilize the needle tip with alcohol before each hole. Additionally, shake the syringe before each hole to evenly distribute the spores in the solution.

Repeat this process for each jar. After each jar is inoculated, flame-sterilize the needle as described previously for the next jar.

Step #3: Colonization

1. Let the mycelium incubate:

Once all of the jars are inoculated, place them in a dark tote or on a shelf in a closet without direct sunlight (ambient light is fine).

Try to keep the temperature between 70 and 80F. Too high of a temperature (above 81F) will increase the likelihood of contamination, while too low of a temperature (below 60F) will produce no growth.

Make sure the inoculation holes are exposed. Fresh air exchange is important for optimal mycelial growth. Paper towels, however, can be loosely draped over the tops to prevent potential contaminants from falling into the holes.

The substrate will begin to colonize within a couple of days. Keep an eye on them every few days. Important: Watch for any signs of contamination such as odd colors or smells. Contamination can spread rapidly, so remove and dispose of any potentially contaminated jars as quickly as possible.

The jars will gradually turn white with mycelium, spreading out from the inoculation sites. This will take approximately 2-3 weeks.

Once the jars appear fully colonized (i.e. you can no longer see uncolonized substrate), allow the mycelium to consolidate by letting them sit for an additional week.

Step #4: Build the Shotgun Fruiting Chamber

The growing environment will take place in a Shotgun Fruiting Chamber (SGFC), aptly named for the shotgun pellet-like holes all around the container. The added perlite soaks up the water in the air and provides a steady stream of high relative humidity. The holes provide constant fresh air exchange.

1. Build the SGFC:

Take the plastic container and drill ¼" holes on all six sides of the container (including the lid, base, and the four sides). Drill them each roughly two inches apart in a grid pattern. It can help to mark out the holes with a marker prior to drilling.

When drilling, don't press too hard or the container may crack. Remove any plastic shards that may be stuck on the drill hole edges.

2. Add the perlite:

Note: Use coarse perlite only. Coarse perlite absorbs the most water and fine perlite may leak through the holes in the bottom.

Fill the bottom with 1-2 inches of dry perlite, making sure the entire base is evenly coated.

Soak more perlite under running tap water with a colander or strainer. Make sure the perlite is moist, with any excess (dripping) water strained away.

Add the wetted perlite to the first layer. In total, there should be an even layer of approximately 4-5 inches of moist perlite.

Over time, the water will evaporate and increase the humidity of the chamber.

Set the SGFC over four stable objects to elevate it at least two inches (this allows gas exchange from the bottom). Bricks or extra wide-mouth canning jars work well here.

Optional: you can place a small plastic container below the chamber to catch any excess water that may drip during the fruiting stage.

Step #5: Birthing and Dunking

1. Birthing

Note: At this point, the colonized substrate ("cakes") are mostly resistant to contamination, so strict sterile technique isn't needed. However, it's best to be cautious and wash your hands before beginning these steps.

Remove the cakes from the jars by inverting them and slapping the bottom. Rinse the cakes under cold running water to remove the dry vermiculite layer. Note: The cakes should come out relatively easily, but if you're having trouble removing them, you can use a knife to cut around the outside to loosen up the mycelium that may be stuck to the side of the jar.

2. Dunking

Fill up a large bowl or pot of cool water and submerge the birthed cakes inside the water. Place a plate or pan on top of the cakes to totally submerge them (they will float and not fully submerge otherwise). The water will rehydrate the cakes, increasing the chance of a good flush.

Leave the cakes in the water pot for 24 hours, making sure they stay submerged.

Step #6: Fruiting

1. Rolling the cakes

After 24 hours in the water, remove the cakes from the pot and place them on a disinfected surface.

Fill a pan or bowl with a few inches of dry vermiculite.

Roll each cake in the dry vermiculite, fully covering each cake. The vermiculite helps to retain the moisture inside the cakes, which will aid in the formation of mushroom pins later on during fruiting.

2. Take the cakes to the SGFC

Now that the cakes are covered in dry vermiculite, it's time to transfer the cakes to the SGFC.

Place each cake on top of a pre-cut square of aluminum foil so the cakes won't be directly touching the moist vermiculite in the SGFC. Arrange them evenly in the chamber.

Once the cakes are on top of the foil, mist the chamber with a spray bottle and fan the chamber with the lid before closing.

3. Maintain Optimal Environmental Conditions

For optimal growth, the fruiting chamber needs to maintain about 95% humidity. To achieve this, mist the cakes with a spray bottle 4 times a day until they glisten with moisture. Avoid totally soaking them and any pools of standing water.

After each misting, fan the cakes with the lid to displace carbon dioxide with fresh air.

The recommended temperature range for P. cubensis is 73-80F, which can be achieved with a space heater if needed. Lower temperatures will cause slower growth, and below ~63F no growth will occur.

Give the cakes a 12/12 light schedule using the "natural sunlight" 6500K fluorescent bulb. Light the chamber from an angle or from above if the lid is transparent. Do not light from inside the chamber, or the cakes may get scorched.

How Long Do Mushrooms Take to Grow?

Anywhere from 5-14 days later, mushrooms will begin to form. They will first appear as tiny bumps that will grow into pins. With each passing day, they will roughly double in size.

The first flush will be ready to harvest right before the partial veil (the thin membrane below the cap) breaks. At this stage, the mushrooms have round caps, covered gills, and are not releasing spores. You can cut or gently twist the mushrooms close to the cake to remove them.

Once all the mushrooms have been harvested from a cake, keep the cake dry for a day and then dunk it in a bowl of water for 24 hours. From here, the rehydrated cake can be placed back in the SGFC for another flush. Subsequent flushes don't require another dry vermiculite roll since the vermiculite from the first flush will be ingrained in the mycelium. Using this method, some people report having a total of four flushes from each cake, however, the largest yield will typically be the first and second flush.

Overall, from inoculation to harvest, the PF Tek method will take approximately 5-6 weeks. A well-inoculated cake can create up to 200g of fresh mushrooms over several flushes.

Benefits of Using a Magic Mushroom Grow Kit

Beginners looking to grow magic mushrooms may find magic mushroom grow kits are an attractive option for their ease and simplicity. Grow kits are ready-to-go packs consisting of the fully-colonized substrate and grow instructions. With the right humidity, temperature, and some indirect sunlight, these grow kits are typically harvestable within a few weeks. Let's take a look at some of the pros and cons of this foolproof method.

Pros:

Ease-of-use. Highly simple and hassle-free because they are a ready-to-use, all-in-one package.

Fewer steps involved. You can skip the sterilization, incubation, and colonization steps.

Convenient. Ideal for someone with a busy schedule. Not as much preparation, misting, and fanning are required.

Quicker. If all goes well, grow kits are harvestable in 2-3 weeks. The PF Tek method takes 5-6 weeks in total.

Cons:

More expensive in the long run. Not as cost-effective as buying grow materials in bulk.

Less reliable and prone to contamination. Grow kits can be hard to troubleshoot if problems arise and the sterile techniques used by the company are largely unknown.

Less yield. It may also not be reusable for multiple flushes, depending on the grow kit.

Legality. Unlike spores, 100% psilocybin mushroom mycelium is illegal to ship or possess in many countries.

Grow kits can offer a quick and easy route to their possession, the best bet is to start from scratch. The PF Tek is a great way to grow magic mushrooms, with impressive yields at a very reasonable price. In addition, taking part in the full process from inoculation to harvest allows you to learn a lot more about the mushroom grow cycle. In the long run, it can become a fun new hobby or a stepping stone to larger-scale grows for a wide variety of mushrooms.

Harvest and storage

The veil underneath the cap of the mushroom indicates when the mushrooms can be harvested. When this veil breaks open, it is time to harvest. If you wait too long, the cap will open and release its spores. The substrate and the mushroom itself will become covered in black/purple spores. Although this does not affect the potency of the mushrooms, it is best avoided. Harvesting in stages is an option, but beware of contamination. Always wash your hands thoroughly before harvesting mushrooms. Or even better, wear sterile rubber gloves.

Mature mushrooms can be harvested by grabbing the mushroom by the base, and performing a twisting, counterclockwise motion. Pulling the mushroom straight out of the mycelium with too much force can damage the mycelium.

After harvesting, you can use a small brush to gently brush off any vermiculite or substrate left on the mushroom. However, do not wash the mushrooms.

Drying and storing

Fresh mushrooms can be stored in the refrigerator, but only for 3-10 days (depending on the specie and moisture content). For long term storage, drying them is a better option.

Mushrooms contain about 90% water, so drying them is not only an excellent method for storage, it also decreases their size, thus making transport easier. To dry mushrooms, all you need is air circulation and a warm spot. An effective method for drying mushrooms is by placing them on kitchen paper and directing a fan at the mushrooms to provide a constant airflow. At a temperature of 25-30c the mushrooms should be cracker dry in a few days.

Storing dried mushrooms

There are several ways to store dried mushrooms.Most important in order for the shrooms to maintain potency, is to store them airtight and in a dark spot.

Honey. Chop the mushroom up in smaller pieces, or use a jar large enough for the mushrooms to sit in. Make sure you write down the contents (weight) of mushrooms added per unit of honey to avoid dosage mishaps!

Freezer. Freezing dried mushrooms is said to be the best method for long term storage. Make sure the mushrooms are completely dry before freezing them, or they will become mushy and prone to rot. Store them in an airtight container or plastic bags.

Airtight bags/container. Pack the dried shrooms in a (ziplock)bag. Squeeze out all the oxygen and close the bag. Put the first bag in another bag and pack it airtight. Store in a cool, dark spot.

Best Way to Harvest Magic Mushroom

Determining the right time to harvest magic mushrooms can be a little tricky and challenging, especially if this is your first time. For you to enjoy the many benefits and awesome effects of shrooms or magic mushrooms, it is essential that you know the best ways to harvest them. Following specific steps is necessary to ensure that you will be able to harvest magic mushrooms successful. And it is the goal of this article to shed light on the best ways or methods of harvesting magic mushrooms.

Magic mushrooms are easier to harvest when they grow at the same rate and size, however, this is not always the case. You will notice that there are shrooms that look smaller than the others. Because of the different sizes of shrooms, determining which one is ripe for harvest can be quite complicated. Considering some few important pointers is a must before you start harvesting them.

You will notice that there are large magic mushrooms and there are also medium and small-sized shrooms which need more time to grow. Some first-time magic mushroom growers pick the large shrooms first and then harvest the small and medium-sized ones – thinking that the smaller ones are still growing and developing. However, this is a wrong practice. Harvesting larger magic mushrooms while leaving the smaller size ones is not advisable since this will not increase your harvest. Moreover, you are risking contamination of your magic mushroom grow kit.

When is the Best Time to Harvest Shrooms?

The best time for you to harvest your precious shrooms is when their hats have not yet fully opened and you can still see that they have a nice round head. You can also harvest your shrooms or magic mushrooms before the veil breaks. The normal veil breaking time is between 6 to 13 days after seeing the first mushrooms pins popping up from the grow medium or substrate. But of course, this all depends on the strain or variety of magic mushroom. Factors such as temperature, air, and humidity play a big role as well.

Harvesting the shrooms before the veil breaks are advisable since this is the time when the matured mushroom are thinking about their next generation. And so they start releasing spores from the gills – this is where reproduction starts to happen. If you want to make sure that the shrooms that you have harvested are potent, then make sure that you count their age. Take note that the small immature magic mushrooms are proven to be more potent compared to larger shrooms.

If you are planning to make spore print syringe, then it is essential that you harvest or pick the magic mushroom before they start releasing spores. These spores will help you preserve the strain and can be used for further cultivation. For magic mushrooms growers who are planning to cultivate and not consume shrooms, the best time to harvest is when that cap has fully opened. Wait for the cap to form into an umbrella-like shape. This should happen a few days after the veil has broken.

Best Way to Harvest Shrooms

Make sure that you do your research first and acquire more knowledge regarding the sizes and maturity of magic mushrooms. Of course, you also need to make sure first that what you are harvesting is indeed magic mushrooms. Remember that there are mushrooms that are poisonous.

It is also essential that you be careful when harvesting magic mushrooms and make sure that you avoid contamination and infection. Once an infection takes place, your magic mushroom grow kit will become useless or unusable. Be sure that you avoid cross-contamination at all cost. This is why you are encouraged to work in a sterile and hygienic environment.

Wash your hands before you proceed with the harvesting. And make sure that you only use top quality antibacterial soap.

It is also recommended that you use sterile gloves when harvesting. Don't recycle the gloves but make sure that you are using new ones everytime you harvest.

You will then remove the container out from the bag.

Be very careful when grabbing the mushrooms. Use your two fingers and grat it at the bottom of the stem.

It is also necessary that you gently turn the stem and then pull it upwards out from the grow medium or substrate.

Don't worry if you will see some damage to the substrate since this is typical. What matters most is that you stay careful and keep the environment sterile at all cost.

As much as possible, you need to avoid breathing in the kit. Keep in mind that your breath is full of bacteria that can contaminate your mushroom grow kit.

Ask for advice from your fellow magic mushroom growers regarding their best harvest practices. Listening to the advice of other growers will help widen your knowledge regarding harvesting magic mushrooms.

9 798674 910619